Scenic Iceland in Winter
Glaciers *to* Geothermal Fields

25 Grayscale Images with Color Photographs for the
Advanced Colorist

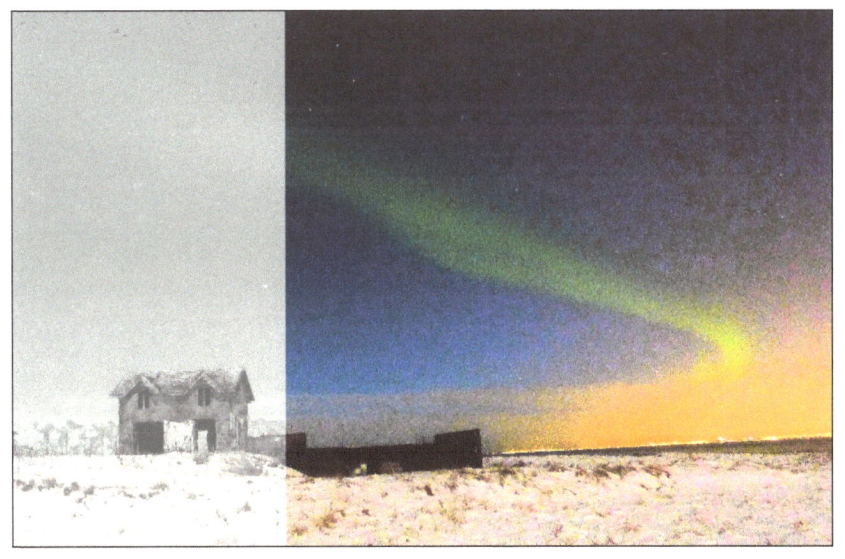

Advanced Adult Coloring Book
GRACE BRANNIGAN

Photographs Elaine Warfield

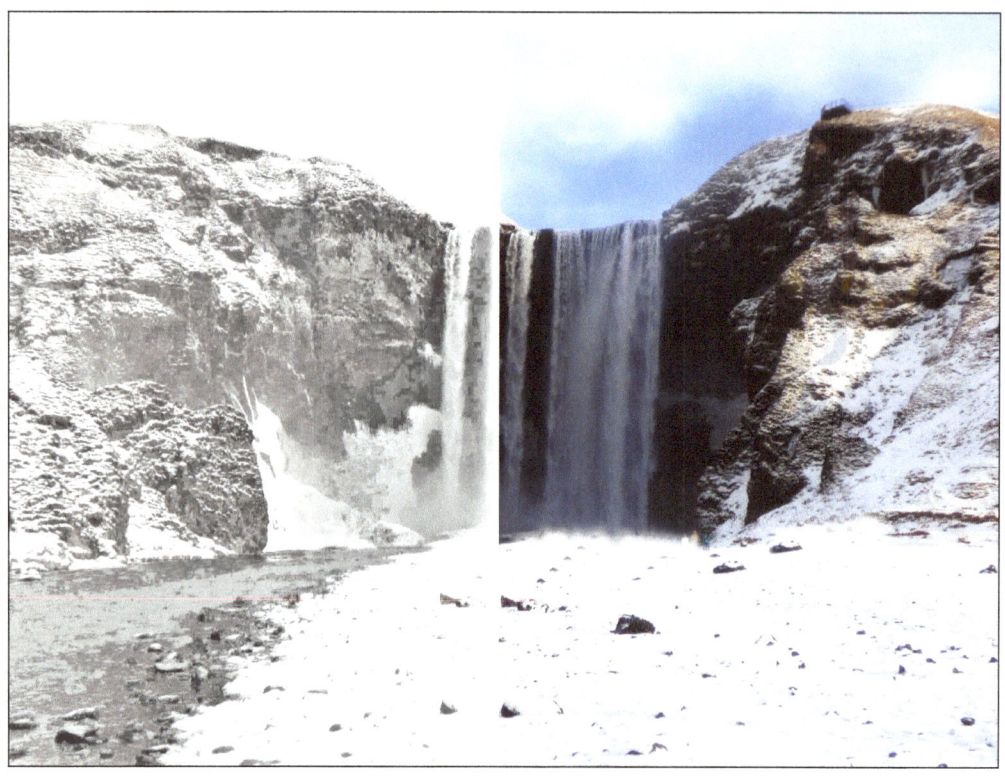

Author Website: http://www.ColoringBooksForAdults.info
Scenic Iceland in Winter: 25 Grayscale Images for the Advanced Colorist, Adult Coloring Book
Copyright 2016 Elaine Warfield
ISBN-13-978-1530319503
ISBN-10: 1530319501
Check out my other coloring books, sketchbooks and journals
Detailed Mandala Coloring Books 1 through 4
Detailed Alphabet Coloring Book: 25 Baroque Grayscale Images
Renaissance Masks: 25 Grayscale Images
On the Go Pocket Size Coloring Books plus Many More...
License Notes
Questor Books, P.O. Box 100, East Jewett, New York, 12424 USA

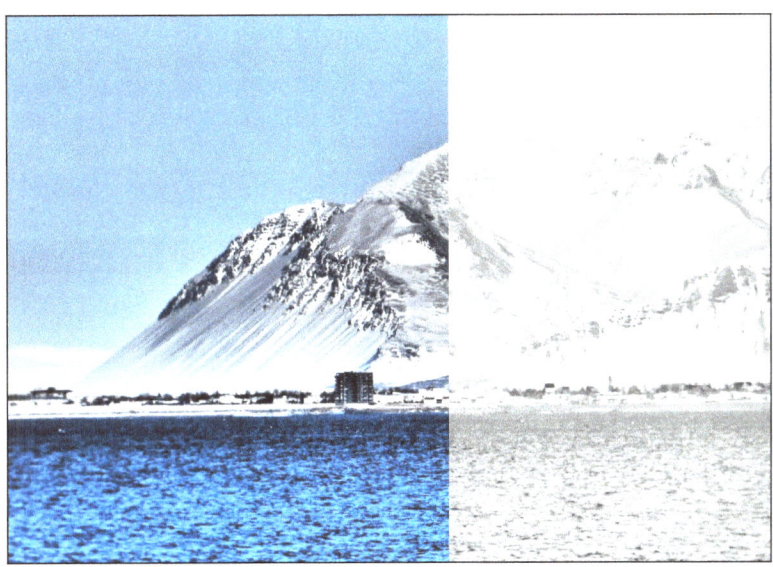

Meditation for the brain -- allow color to soothe you!

This coloring book has 25 photographs in grayscale for Advanced colorists, of scenes from Iceland in Winter. Stunning images for the advanced colorist and those who enjoy grayscale! Please note these images are mostly darker winter time colors of grays, blues and blacks.

∞ ∞ ∞ ∞ ∞ ∞ ∞ ∞ ∞ ∞ ∞ ∞ ∞ ∞ ∞ ∞

How to Color Grayscale: Coloring *Grayscale* images is a fun way to explore and color and it makes shading easier to learn when you follow the shading already in the images. Color dark in the darker shaded areas, then medium and light in the lighter areas. The end result is a uniquely rich and rewarding colored image.

Coloring has been shown to reduce stress and offer meditative release. Create your own visually appealing art using crayons, colored pencils, felt tip markers, ink pens, watercolor pencils, art pencils, gel pens, glitter pens. There is no limit to your creativity and genius. Still not sure? Check out our website online to see some of our colored images. Also, check out online videos on coloring Grayscale.

Please leave a review where you bought this coloring book and share your coloring images. It really helps the author and other buyers. Please visit my Facebook page **Coloring Books for Adults Info.**

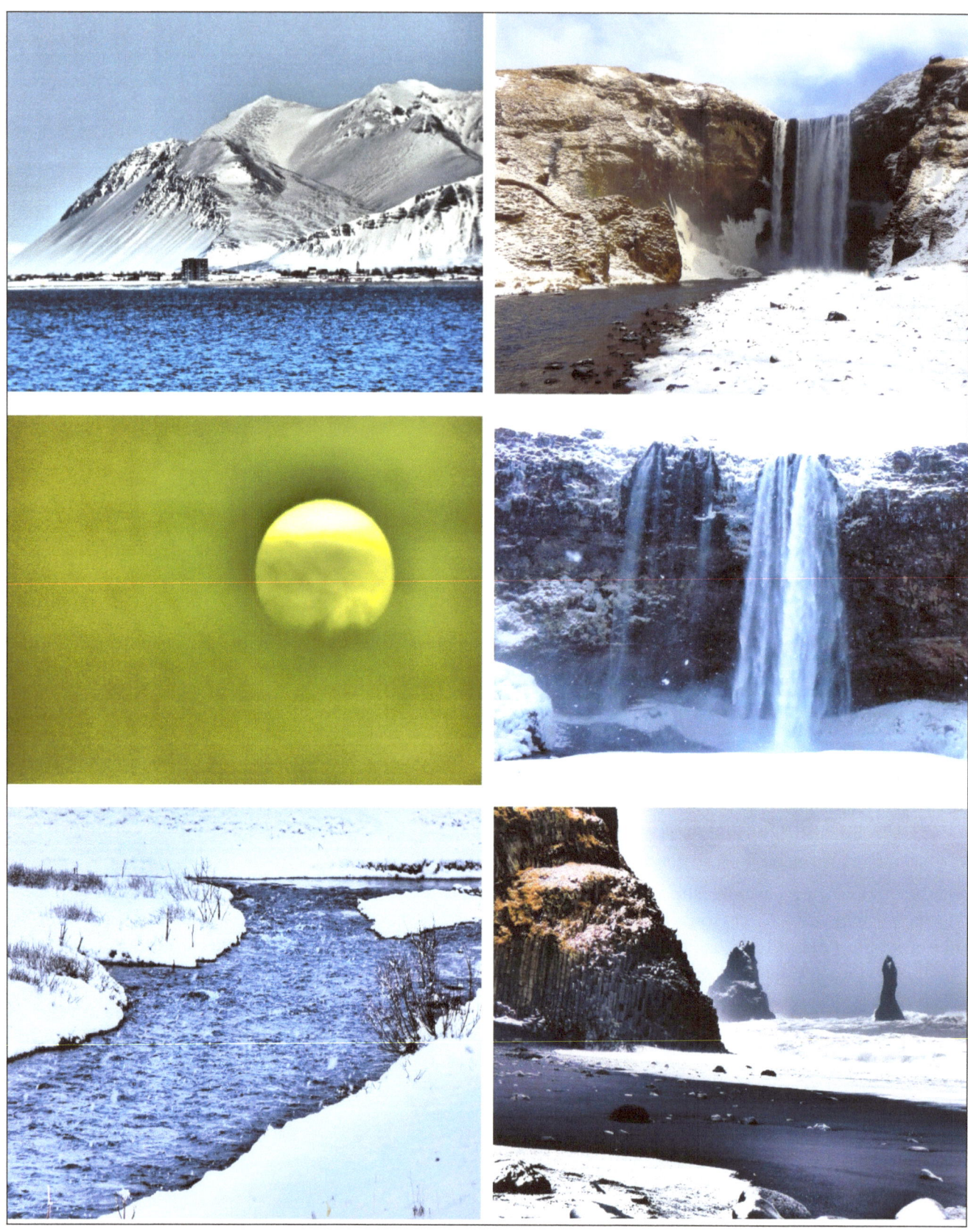

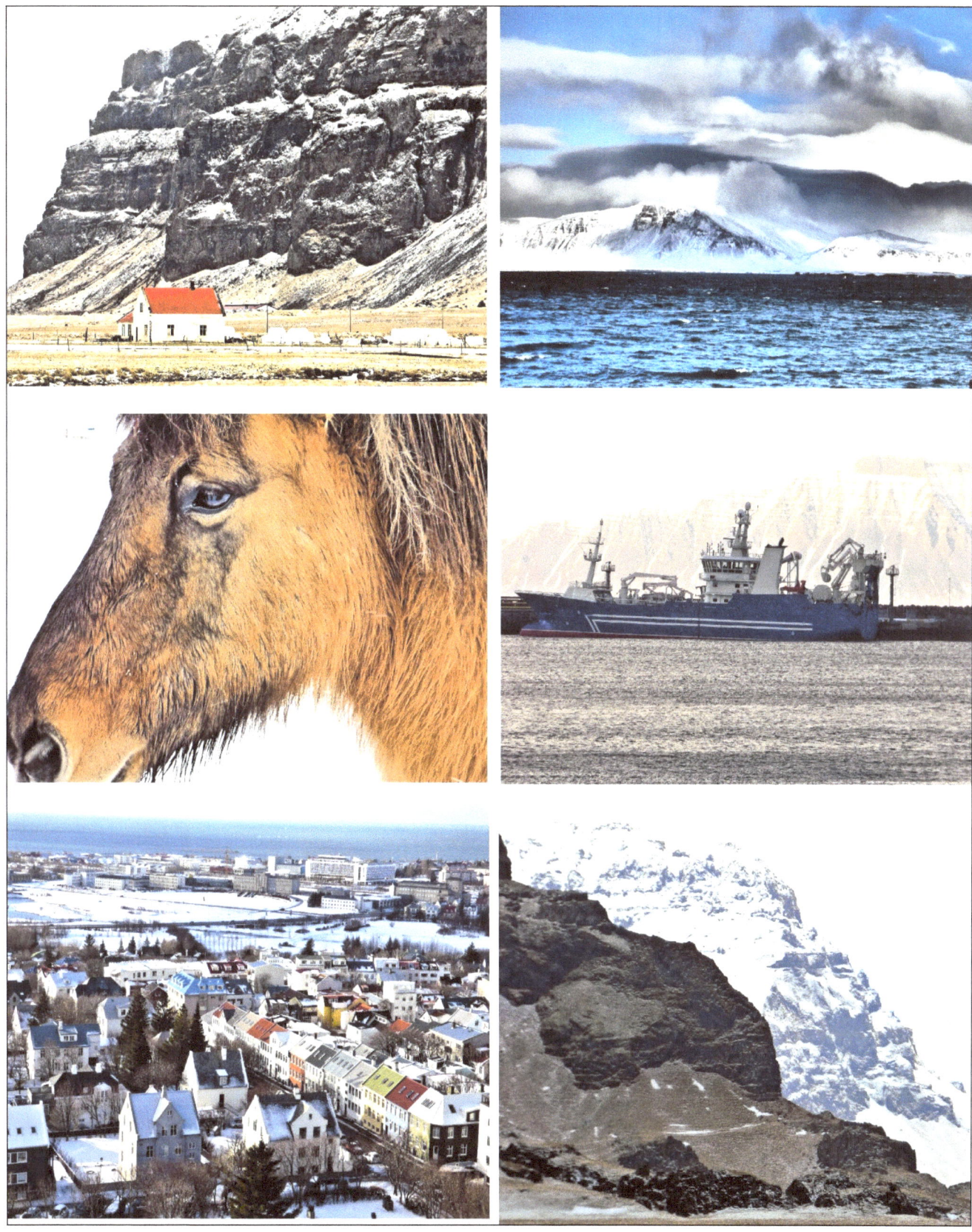

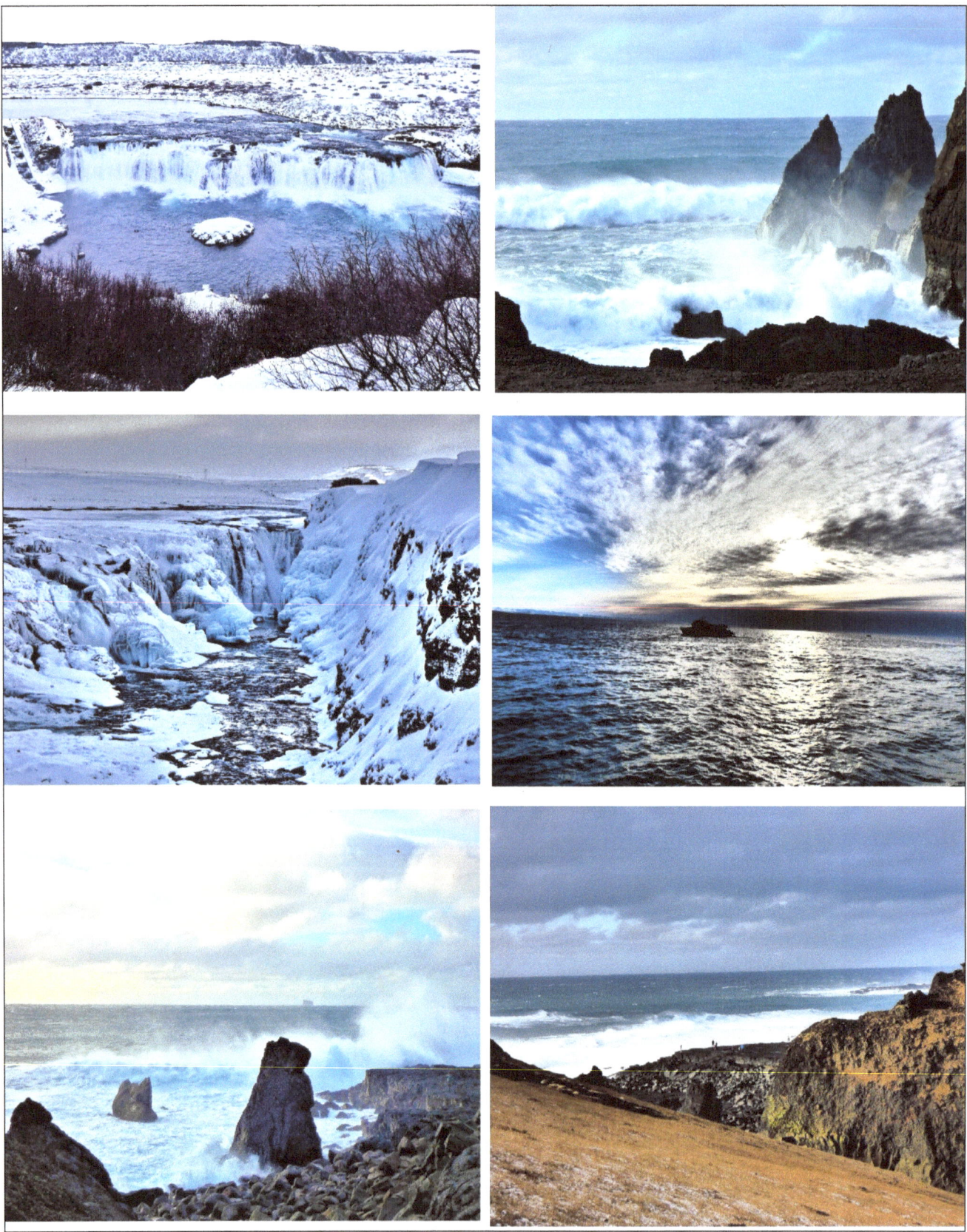

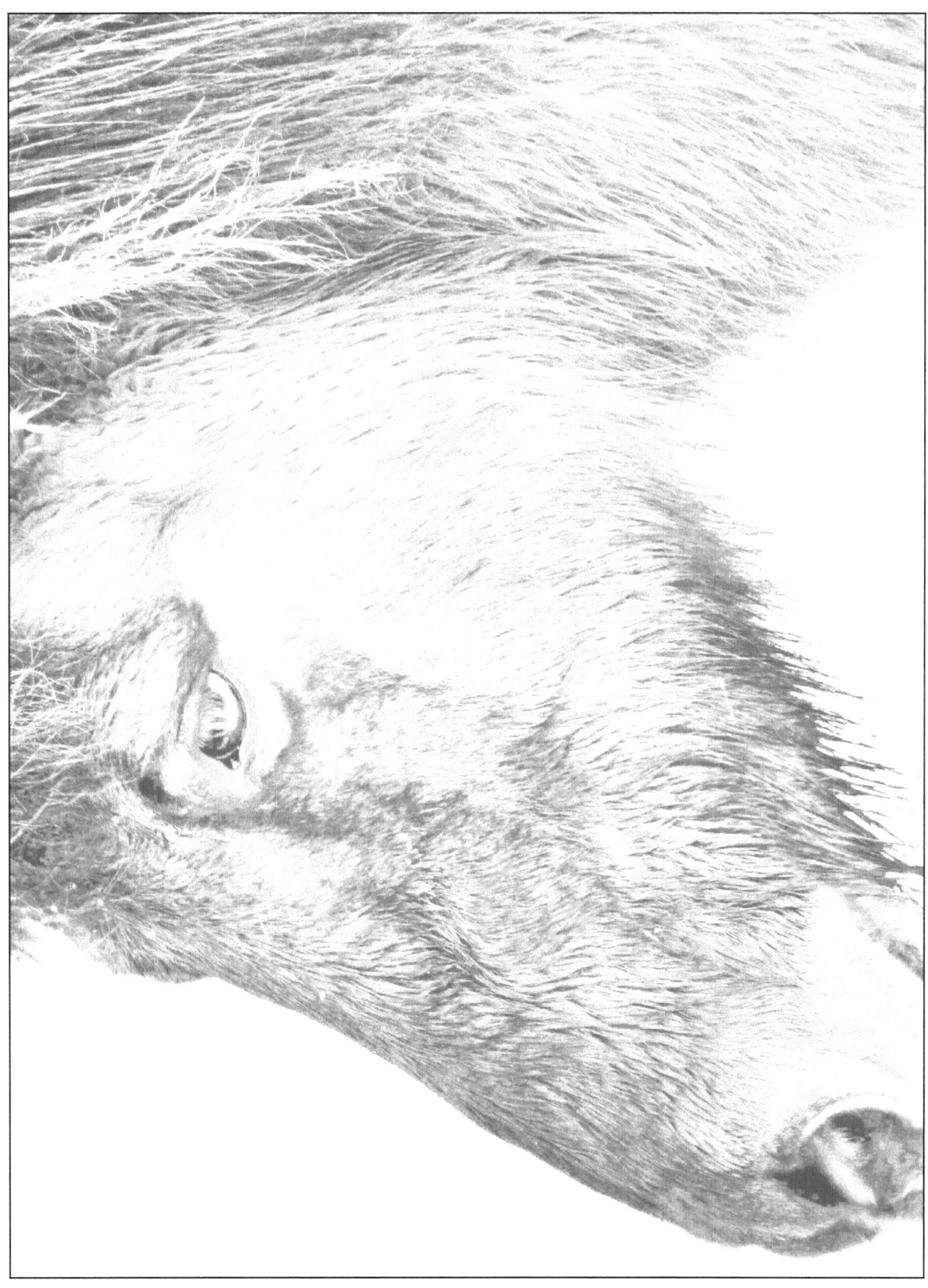

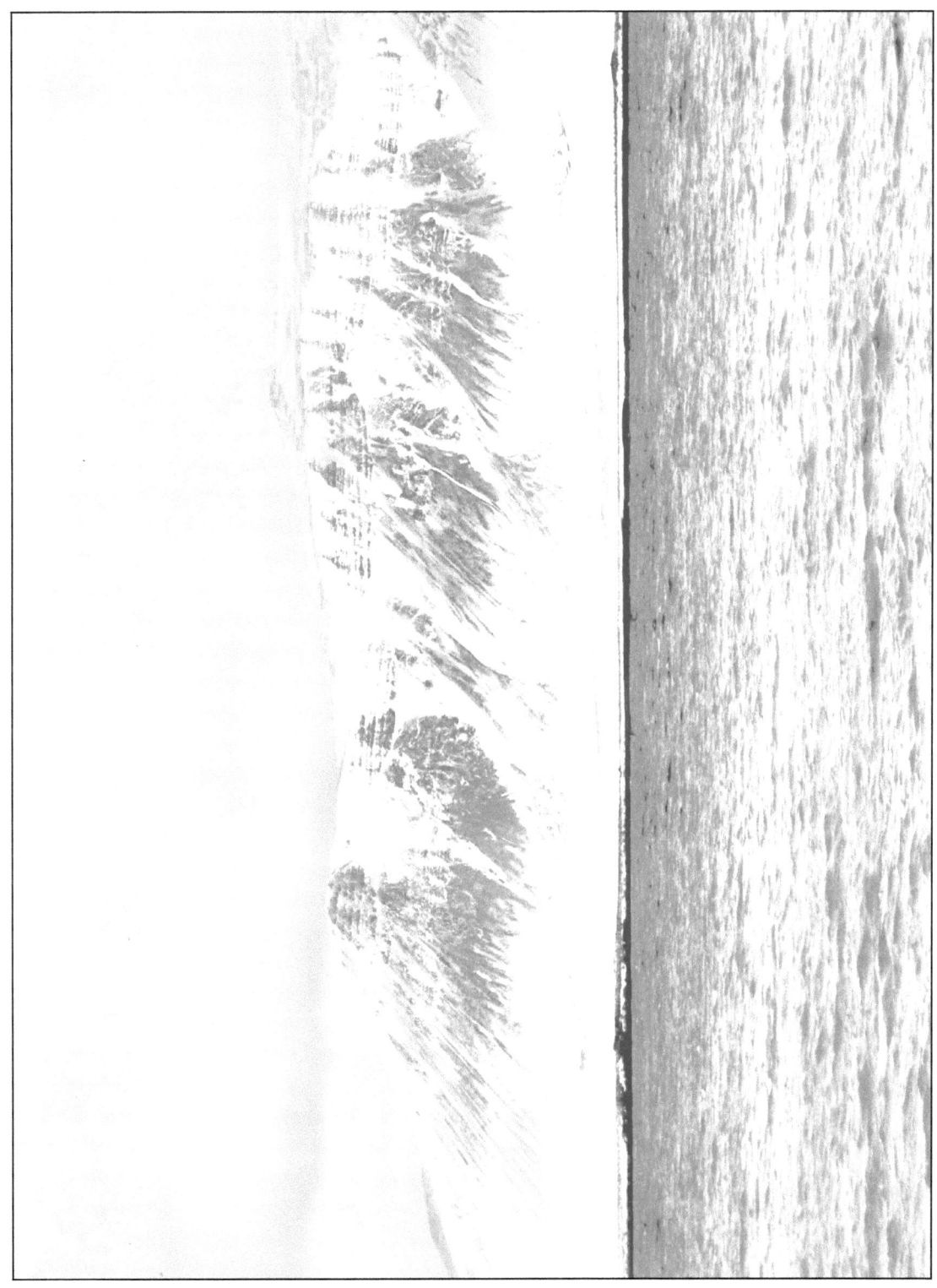

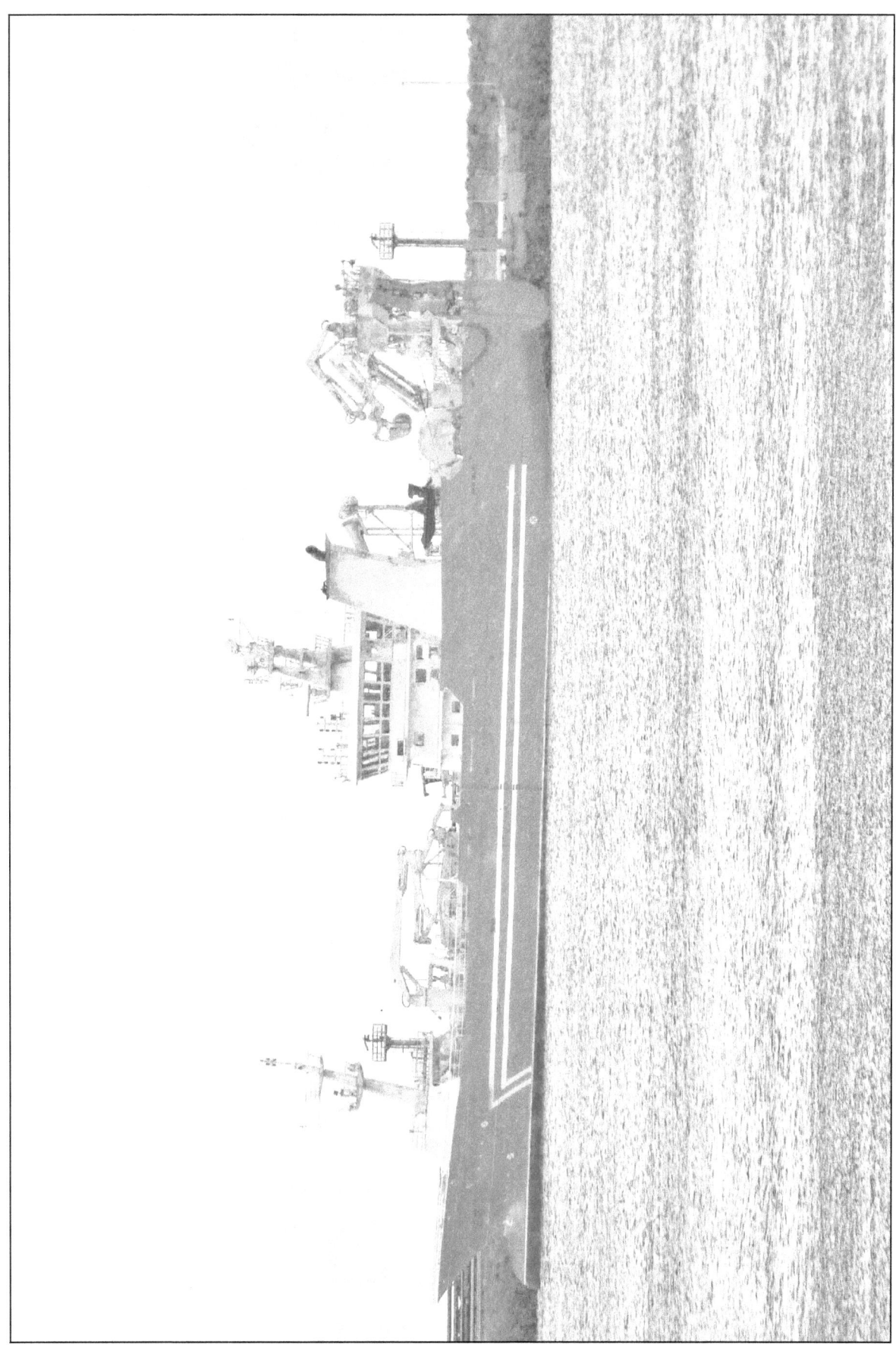

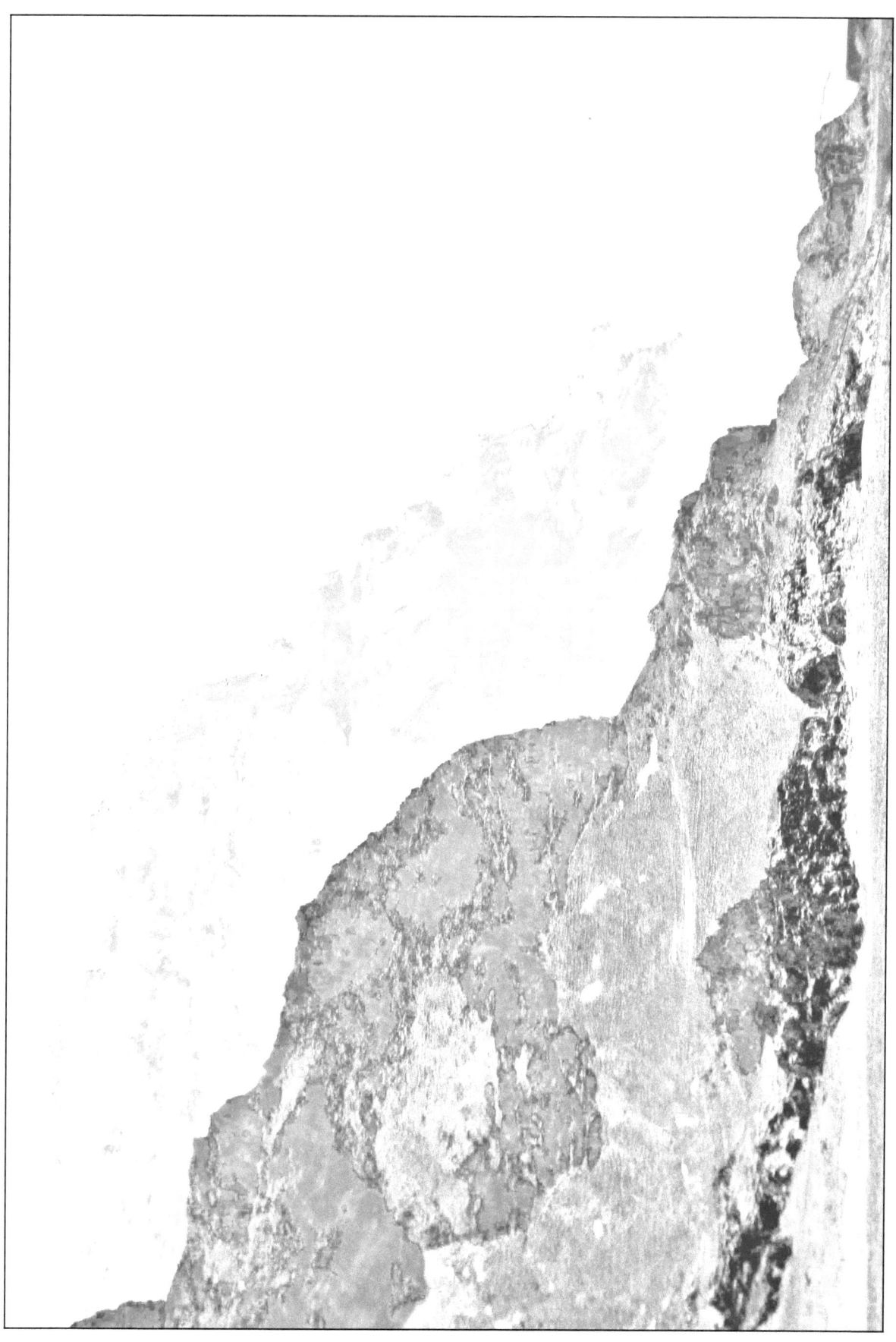

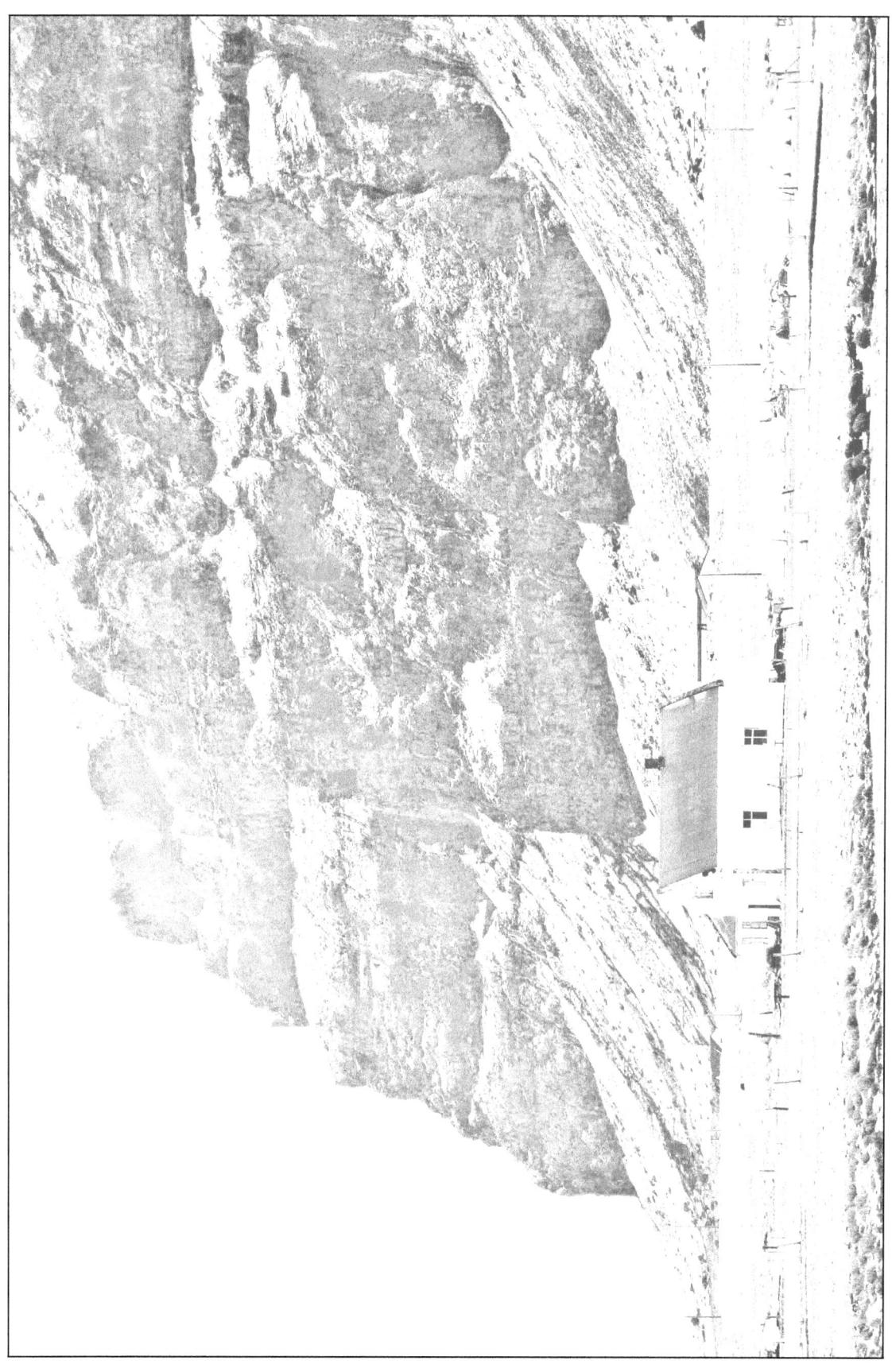

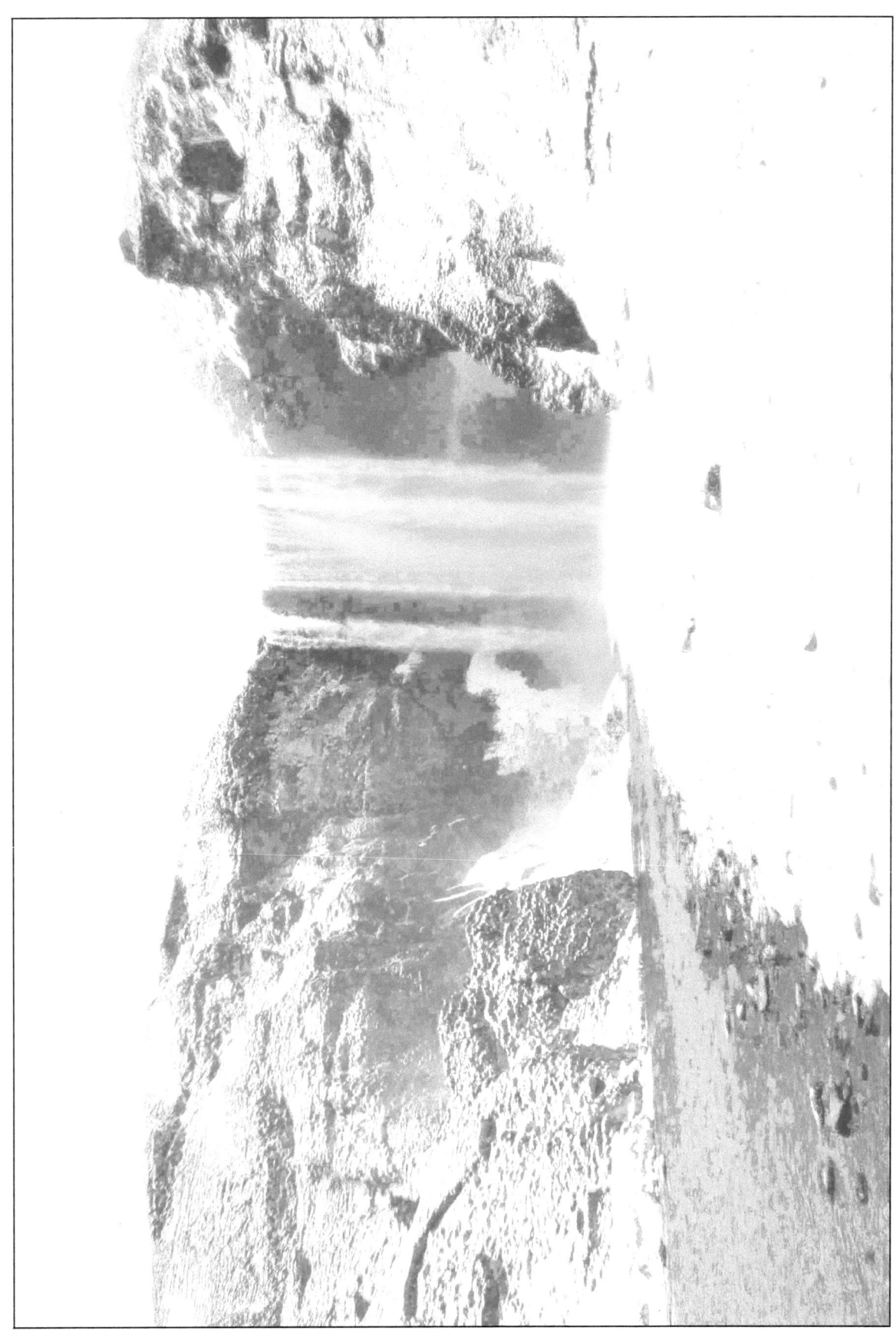

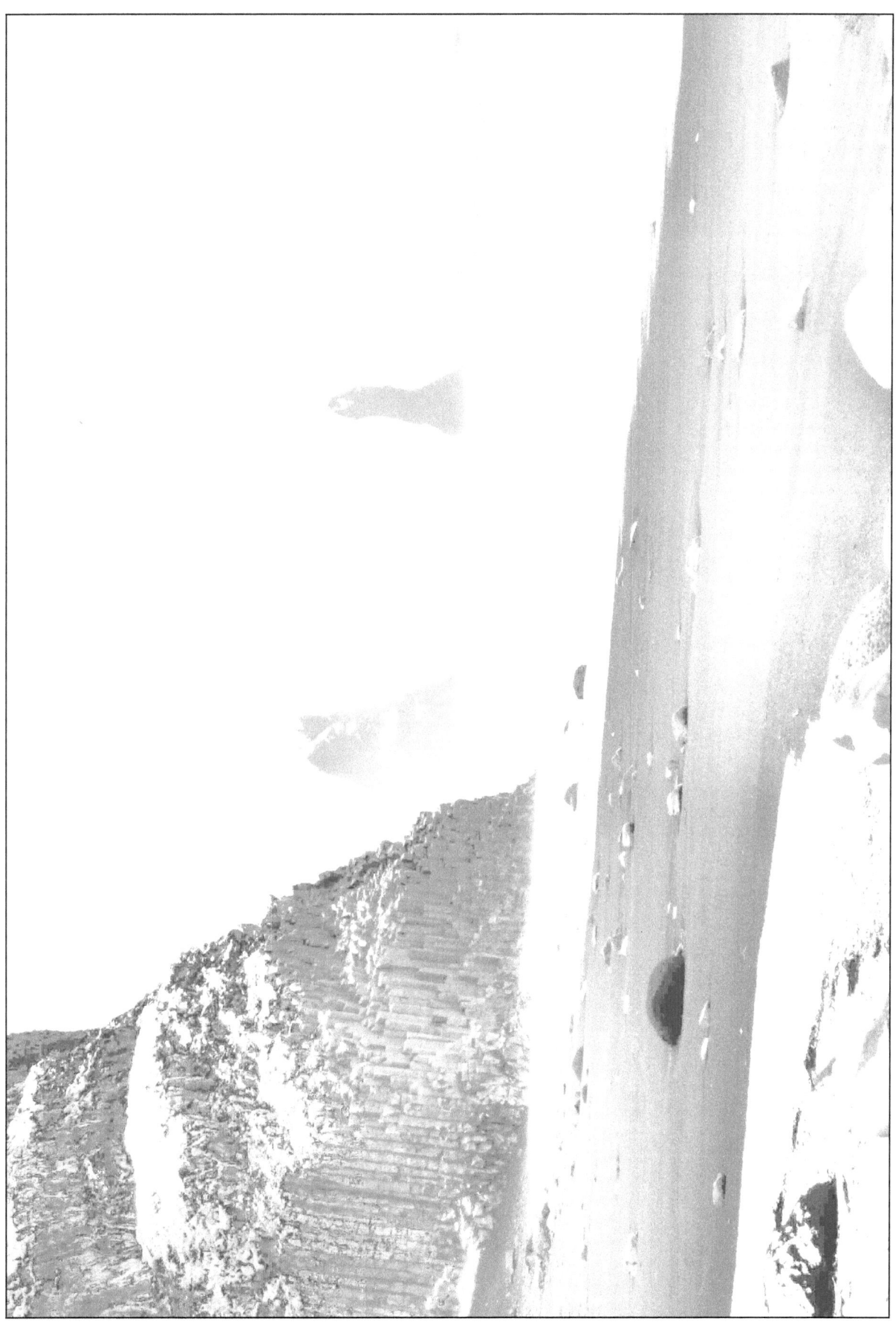

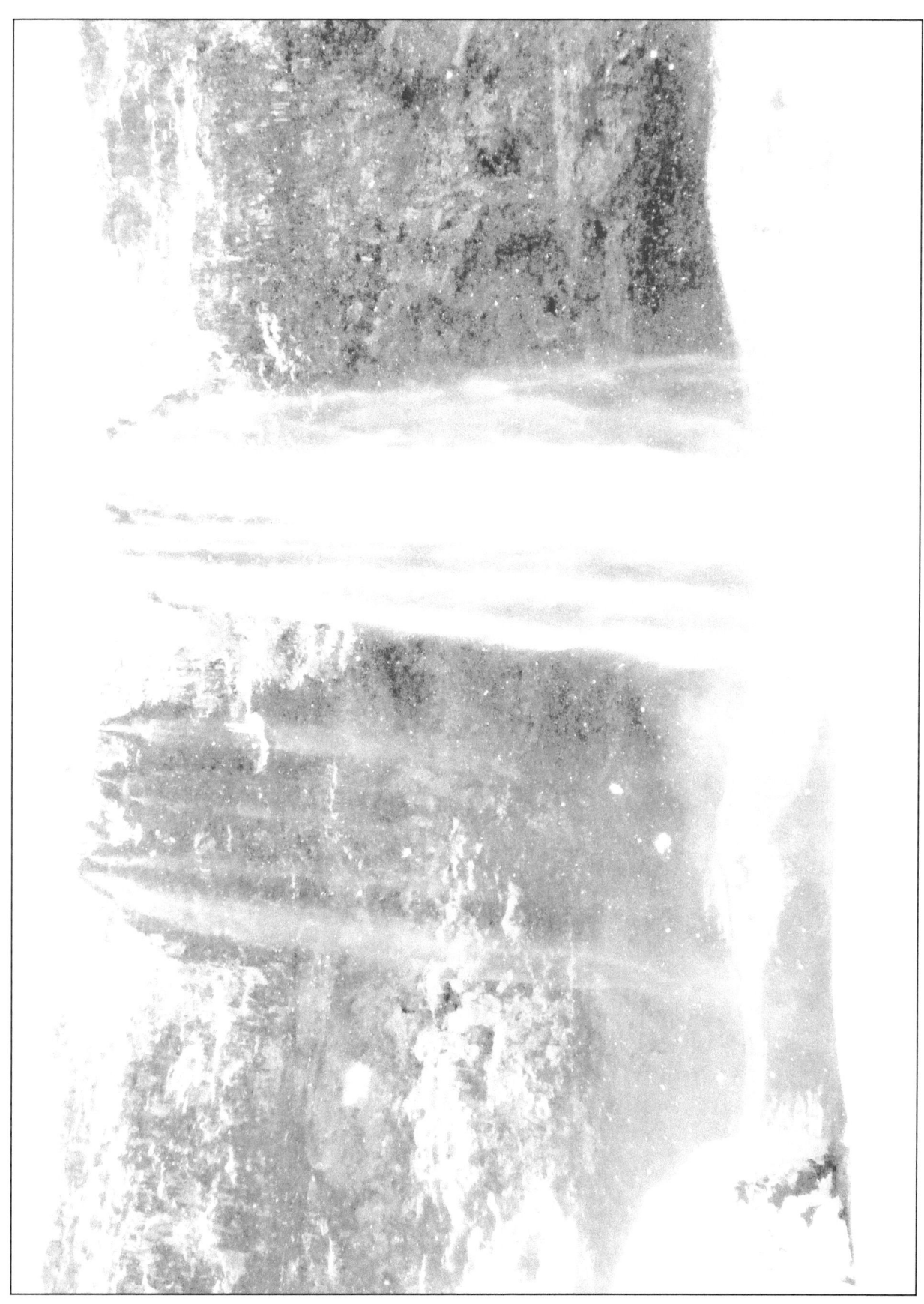

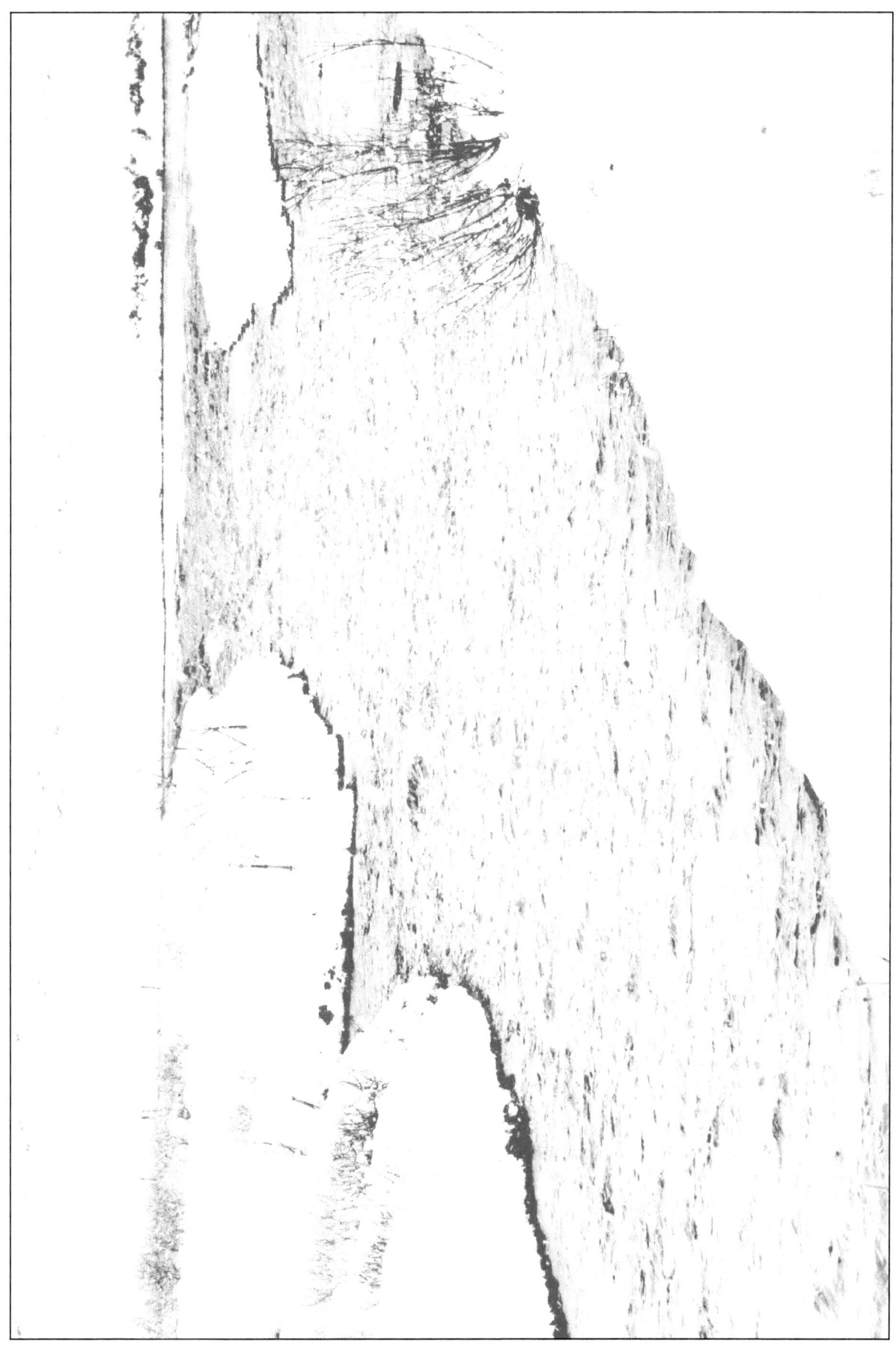

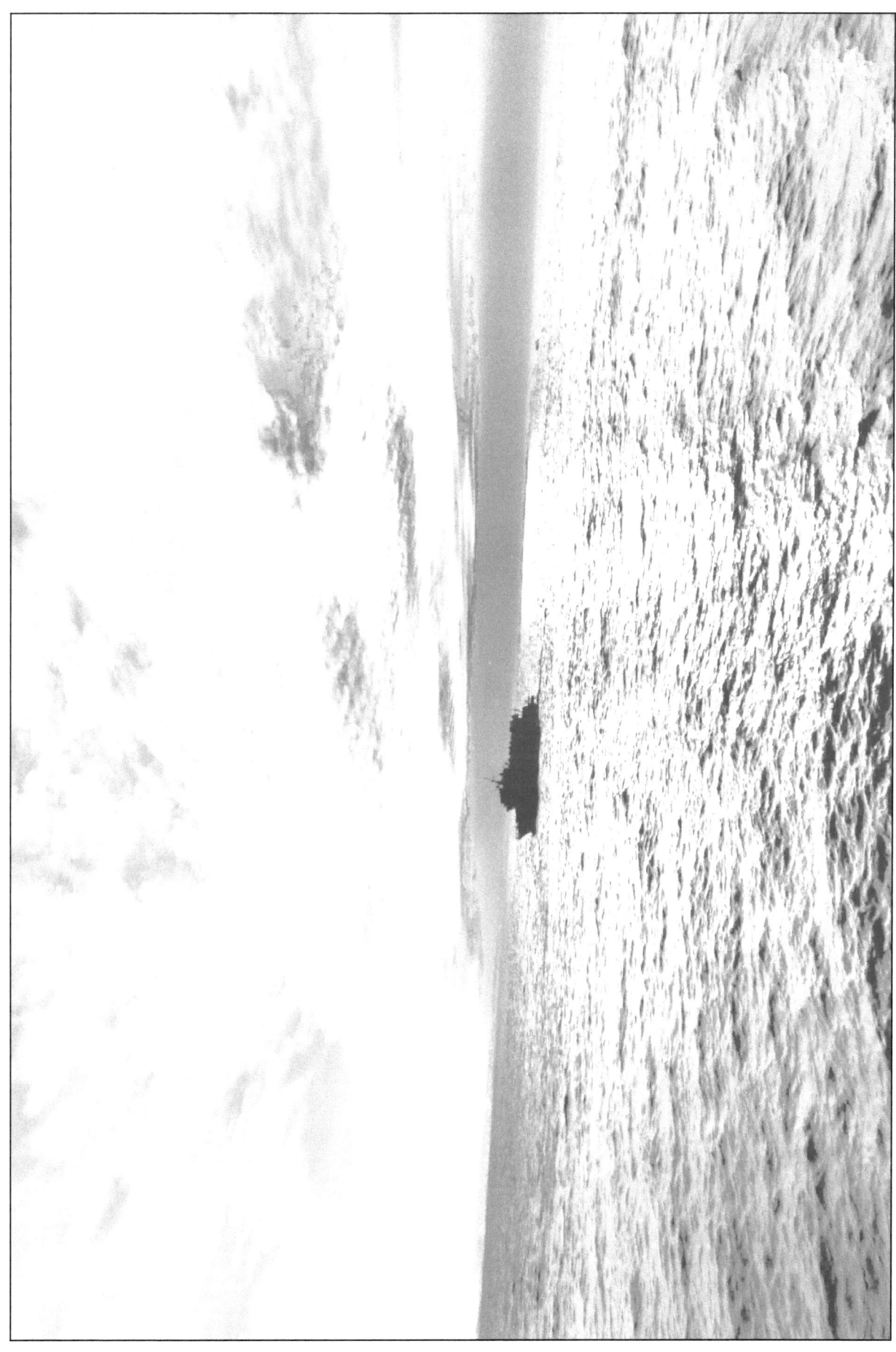

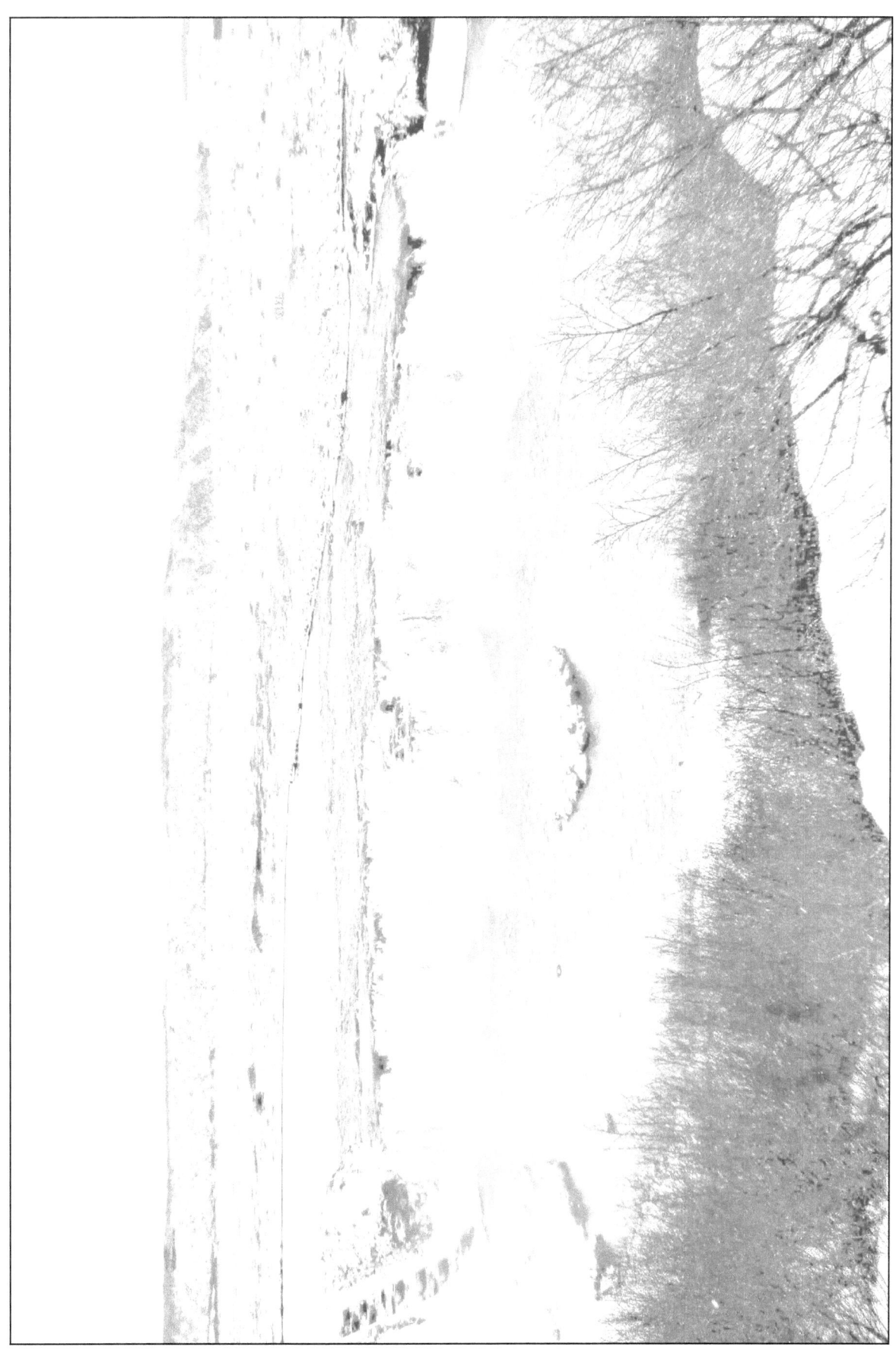

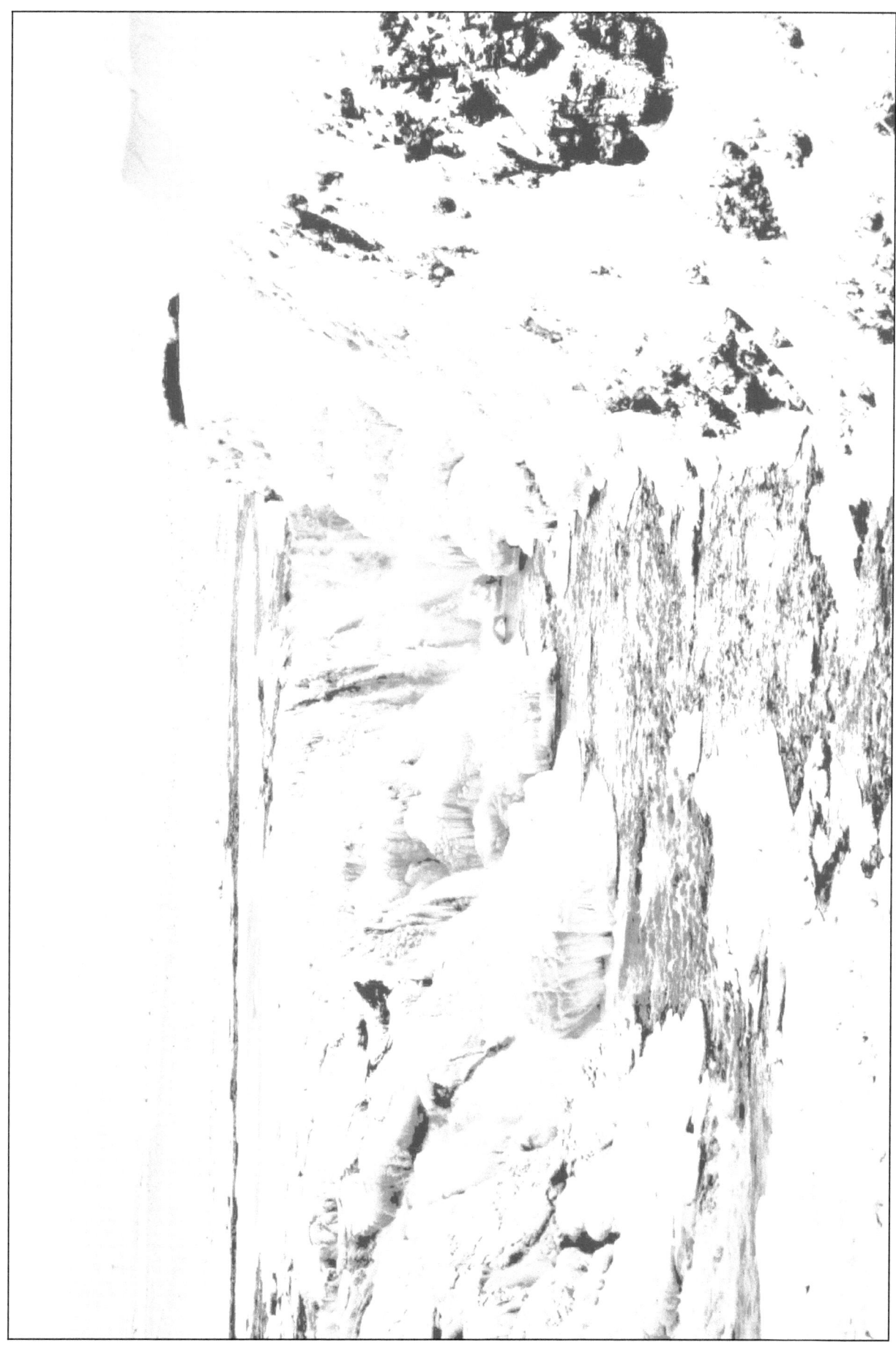

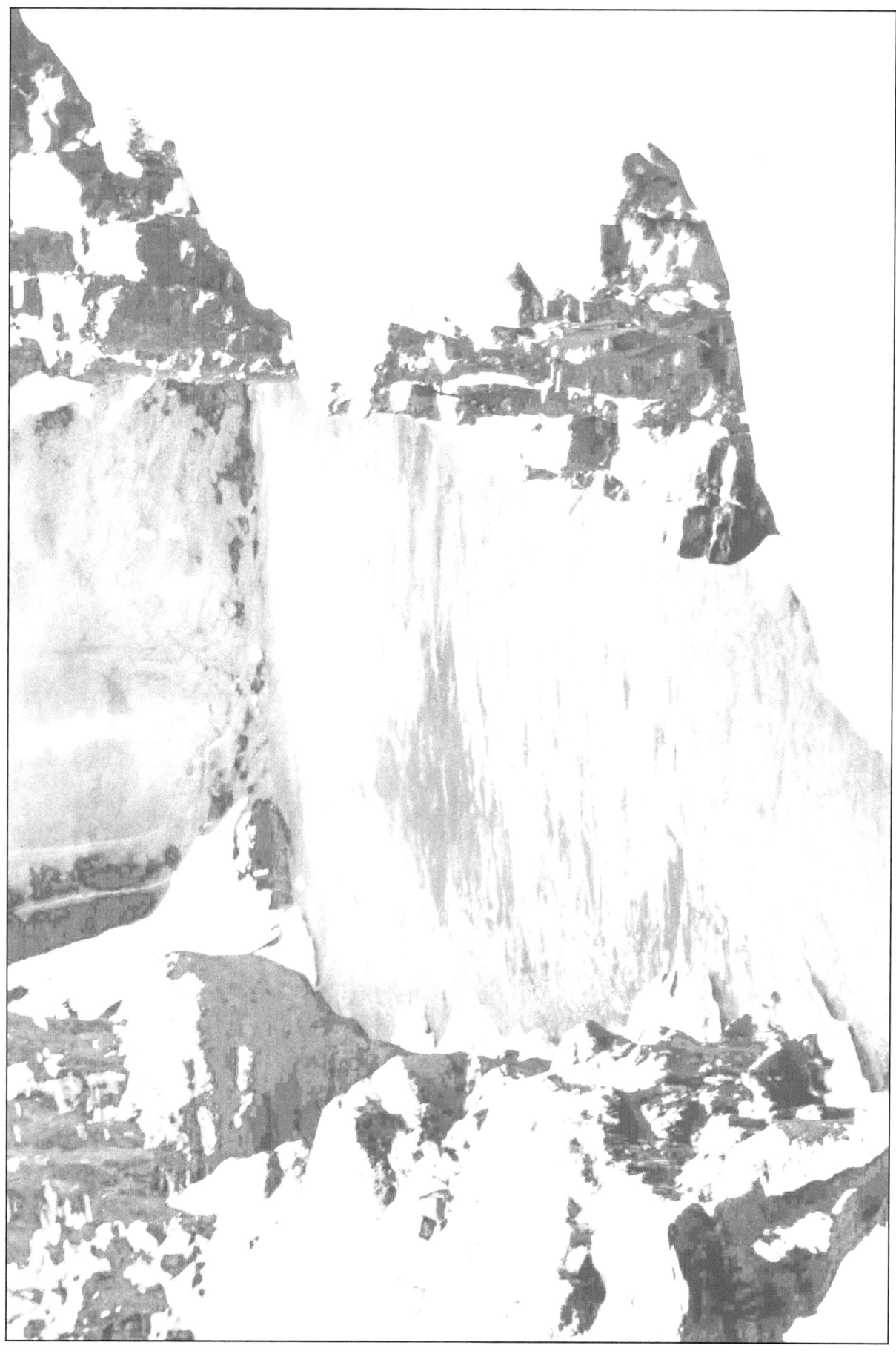

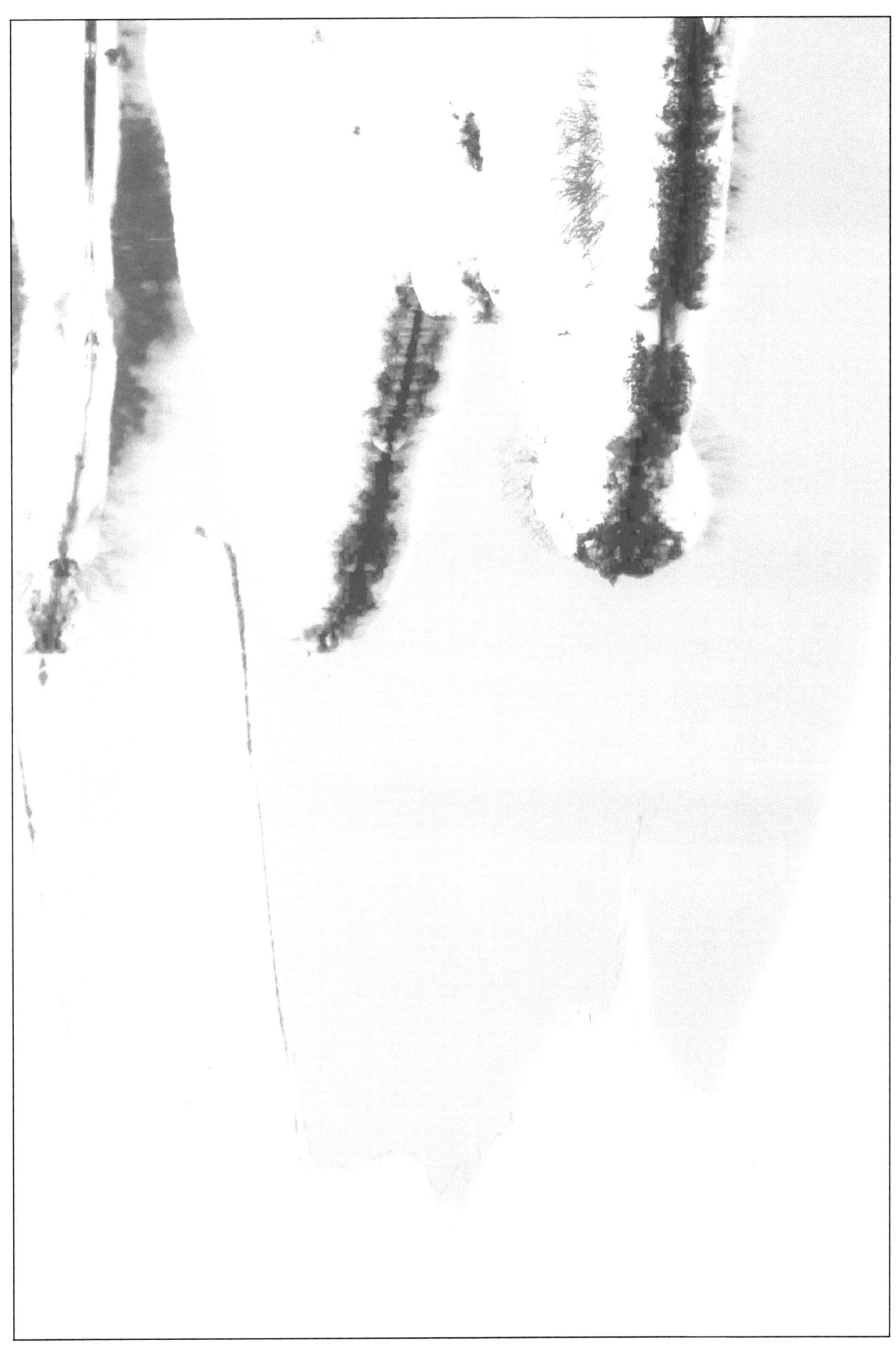

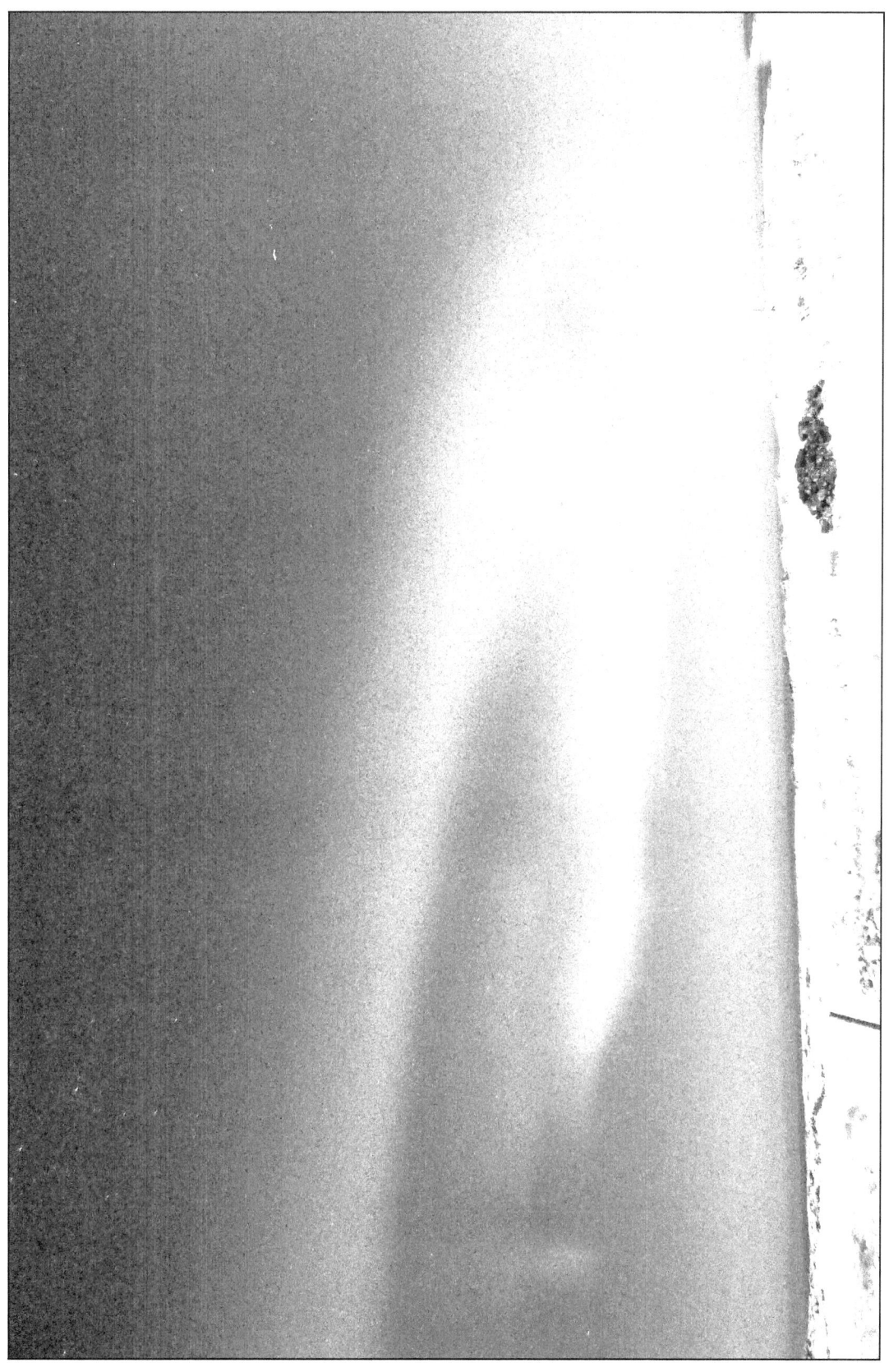

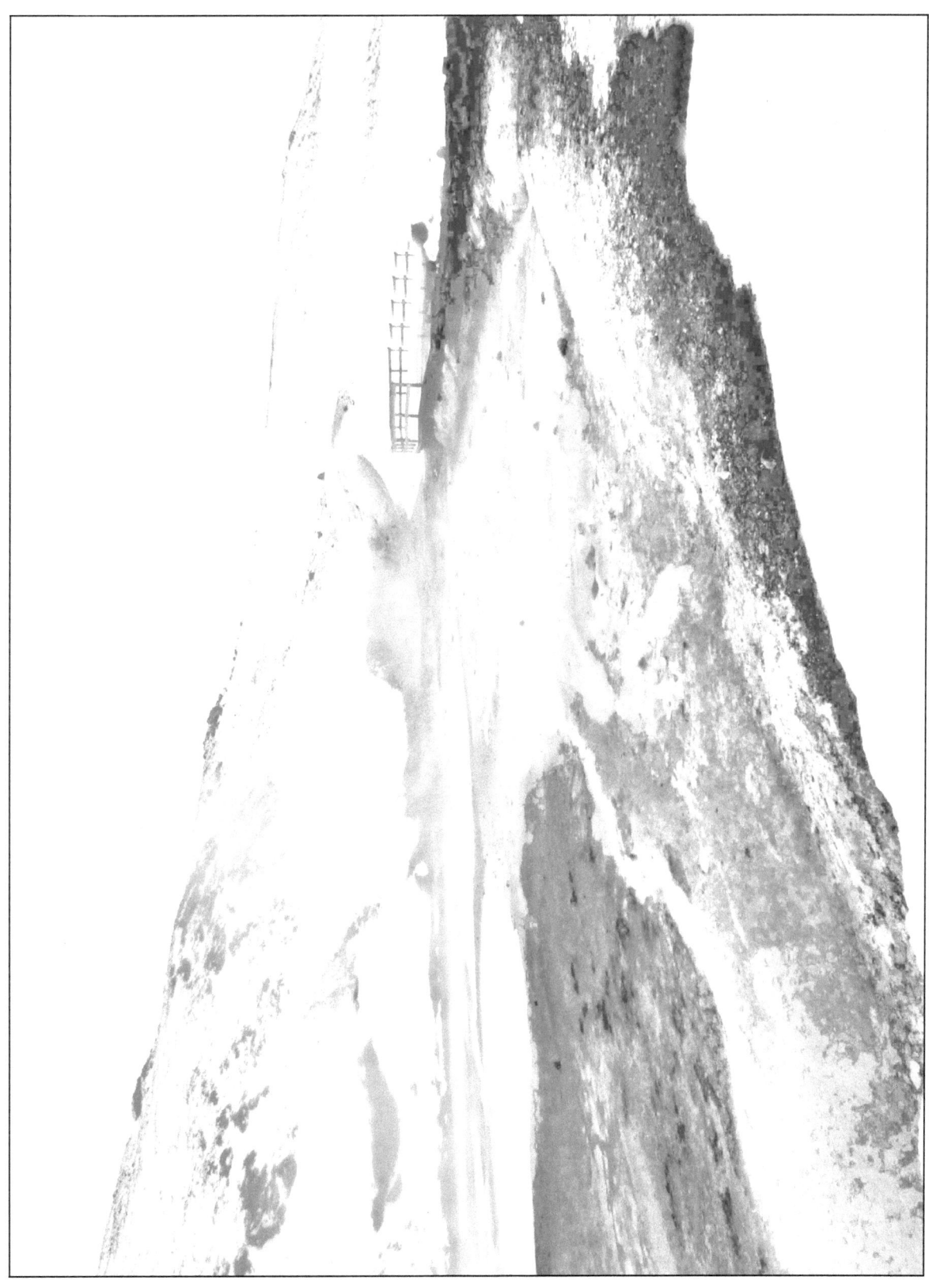

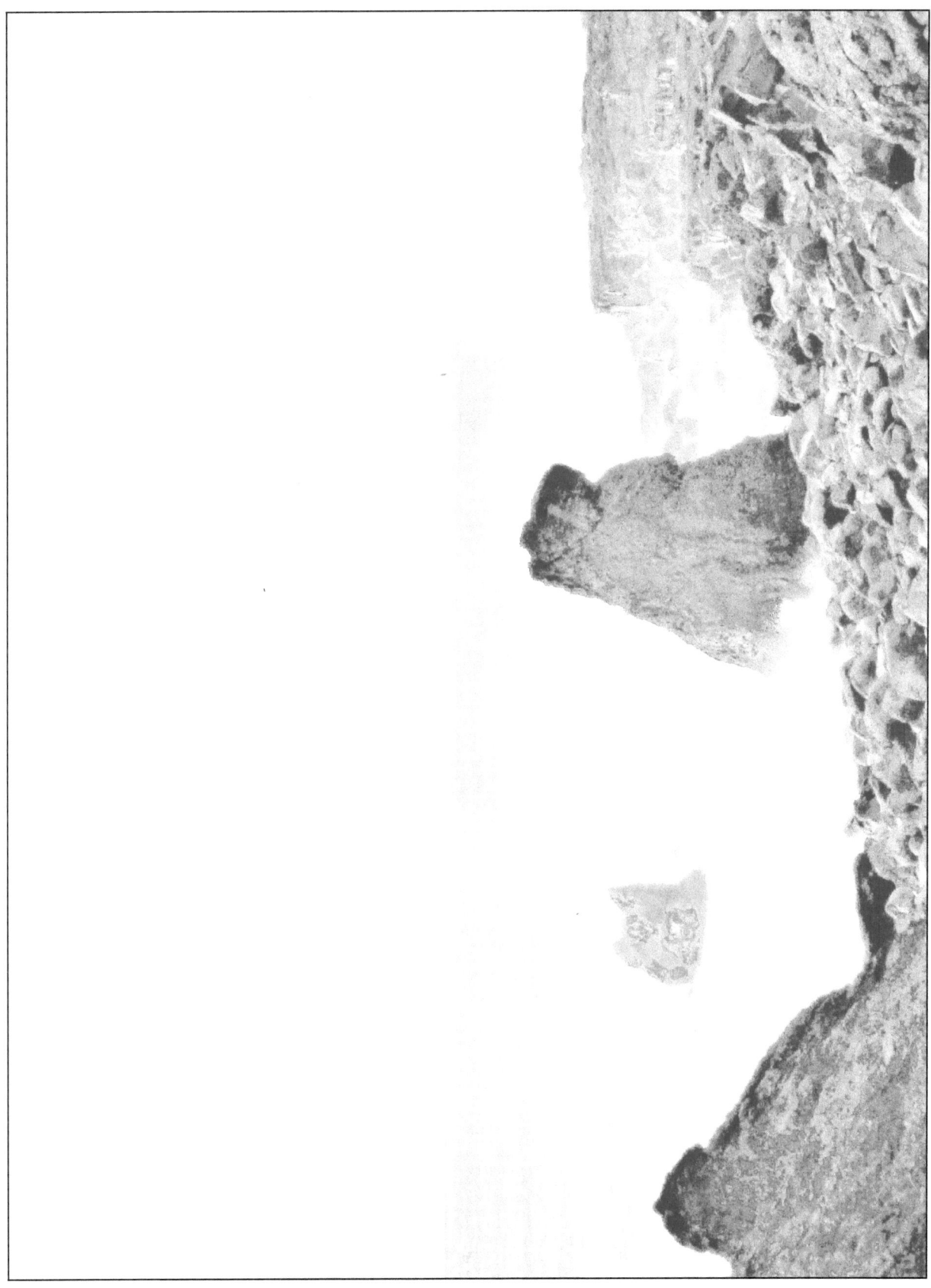

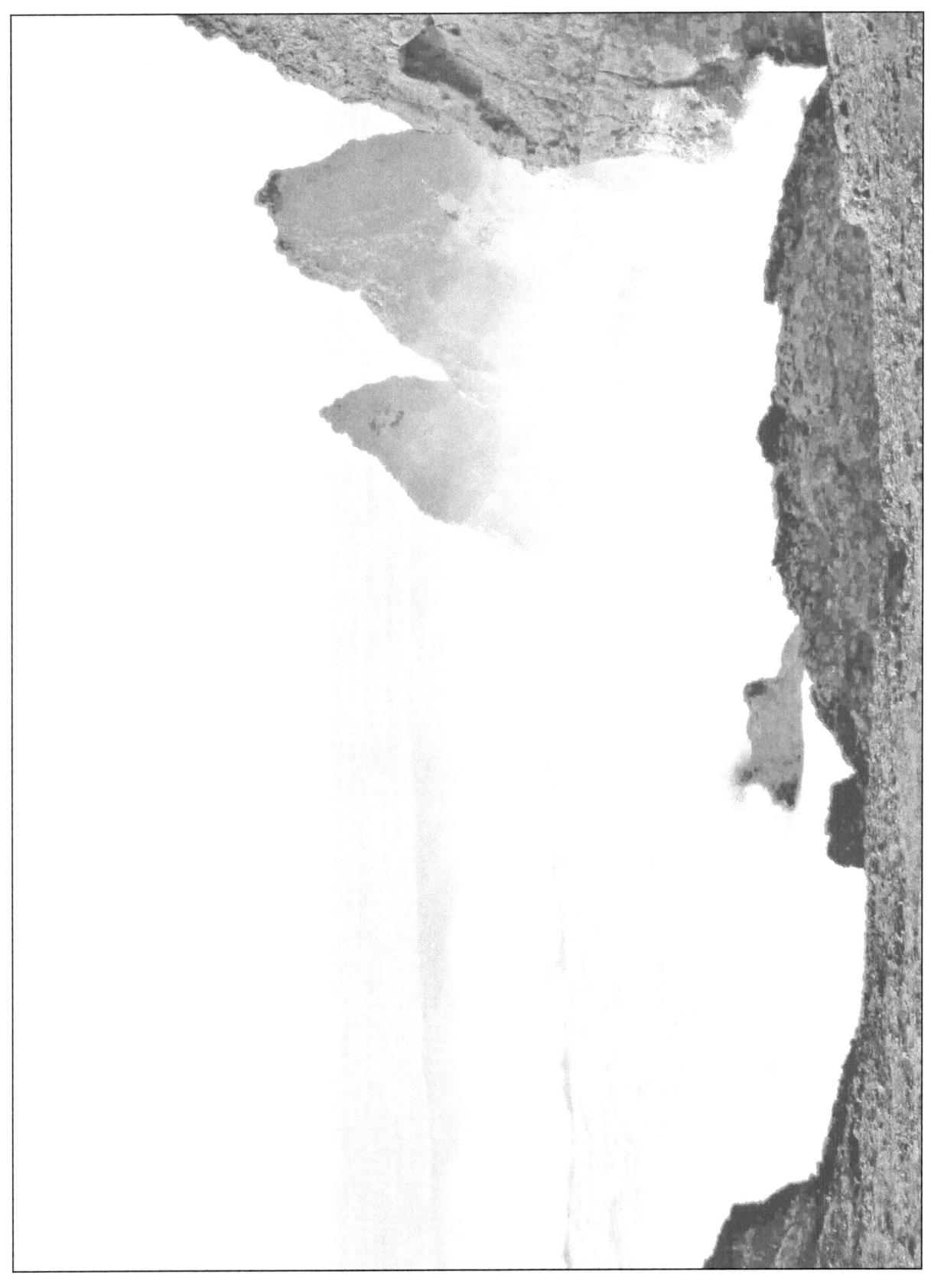

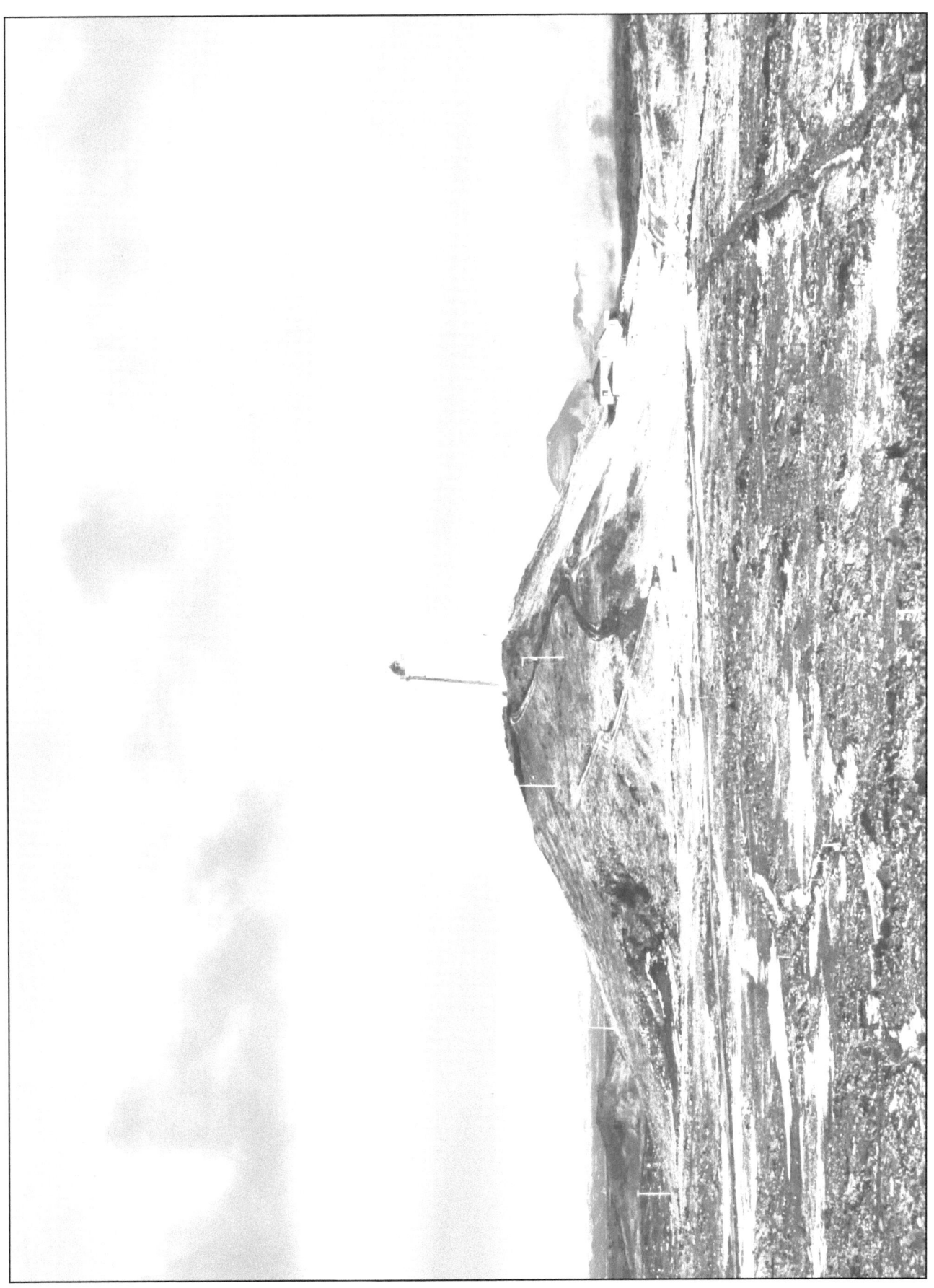

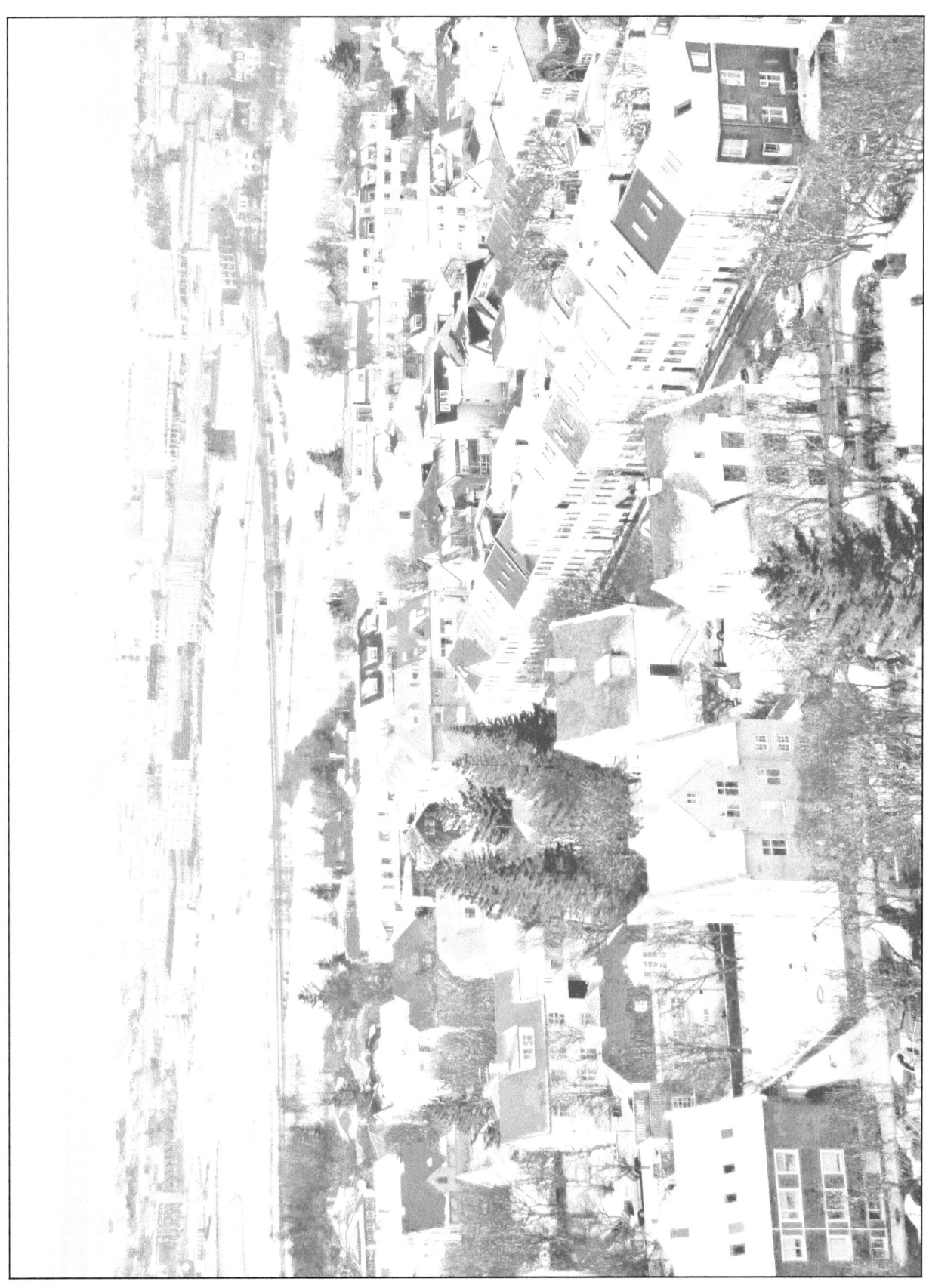

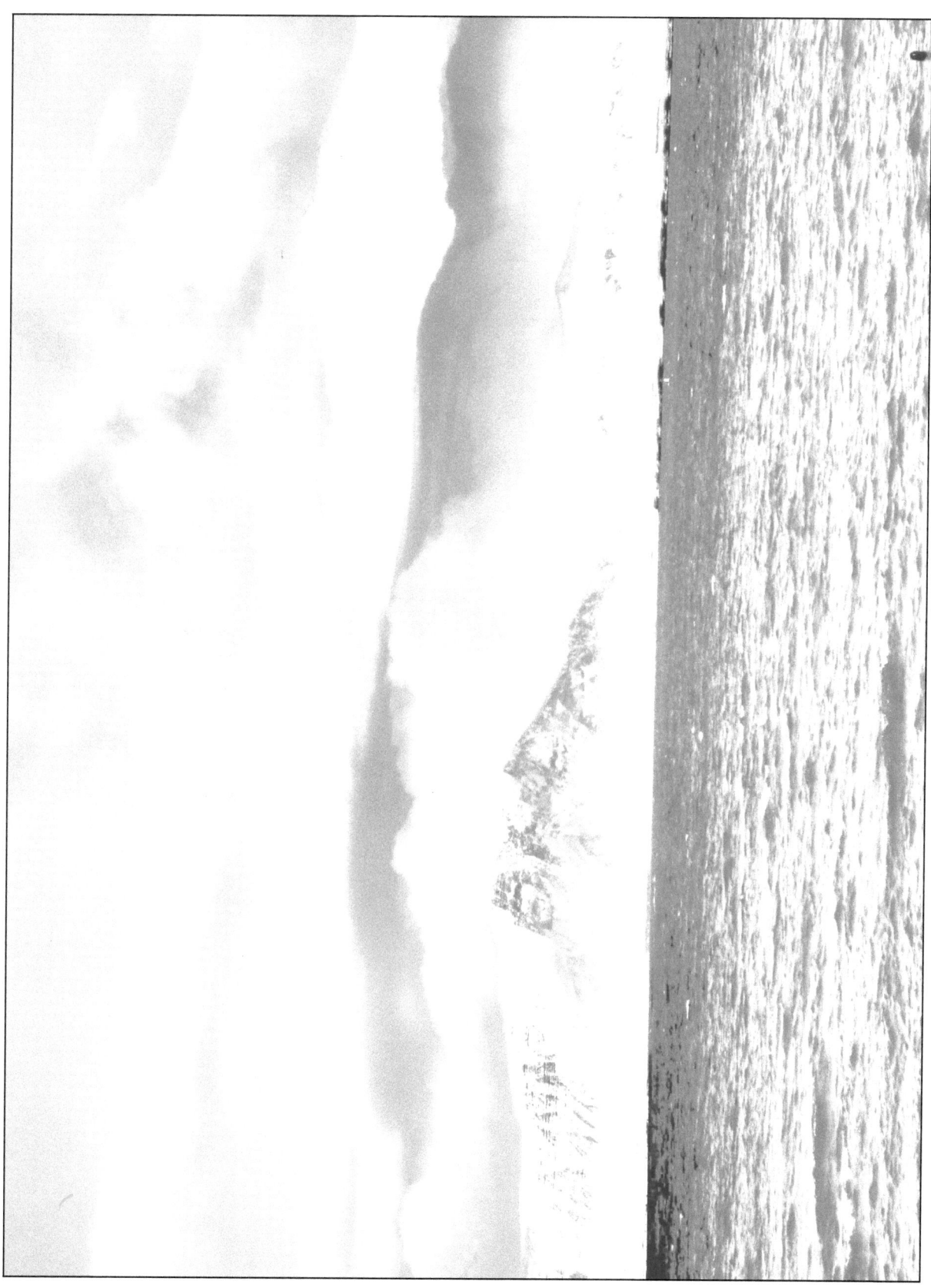

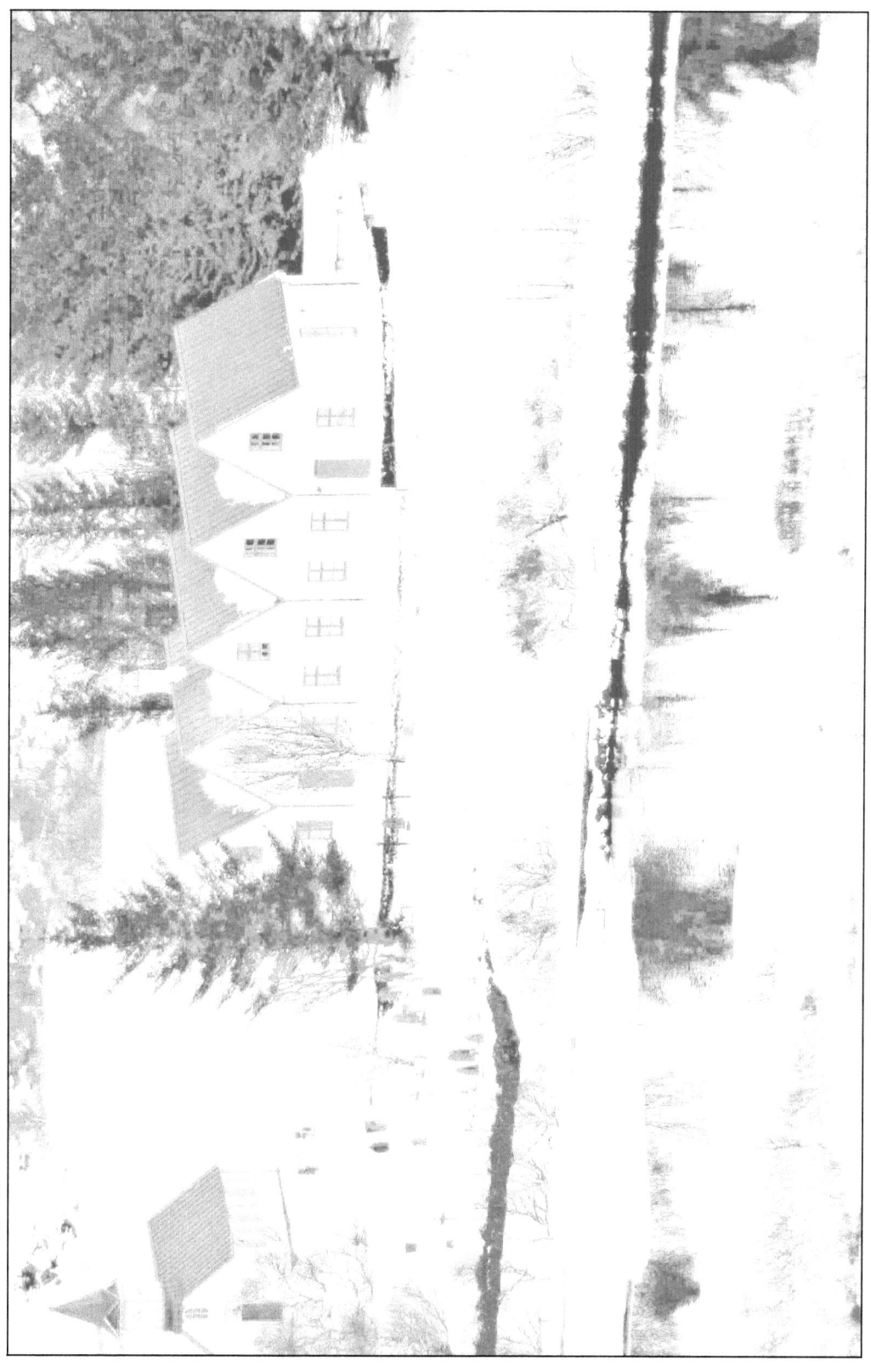

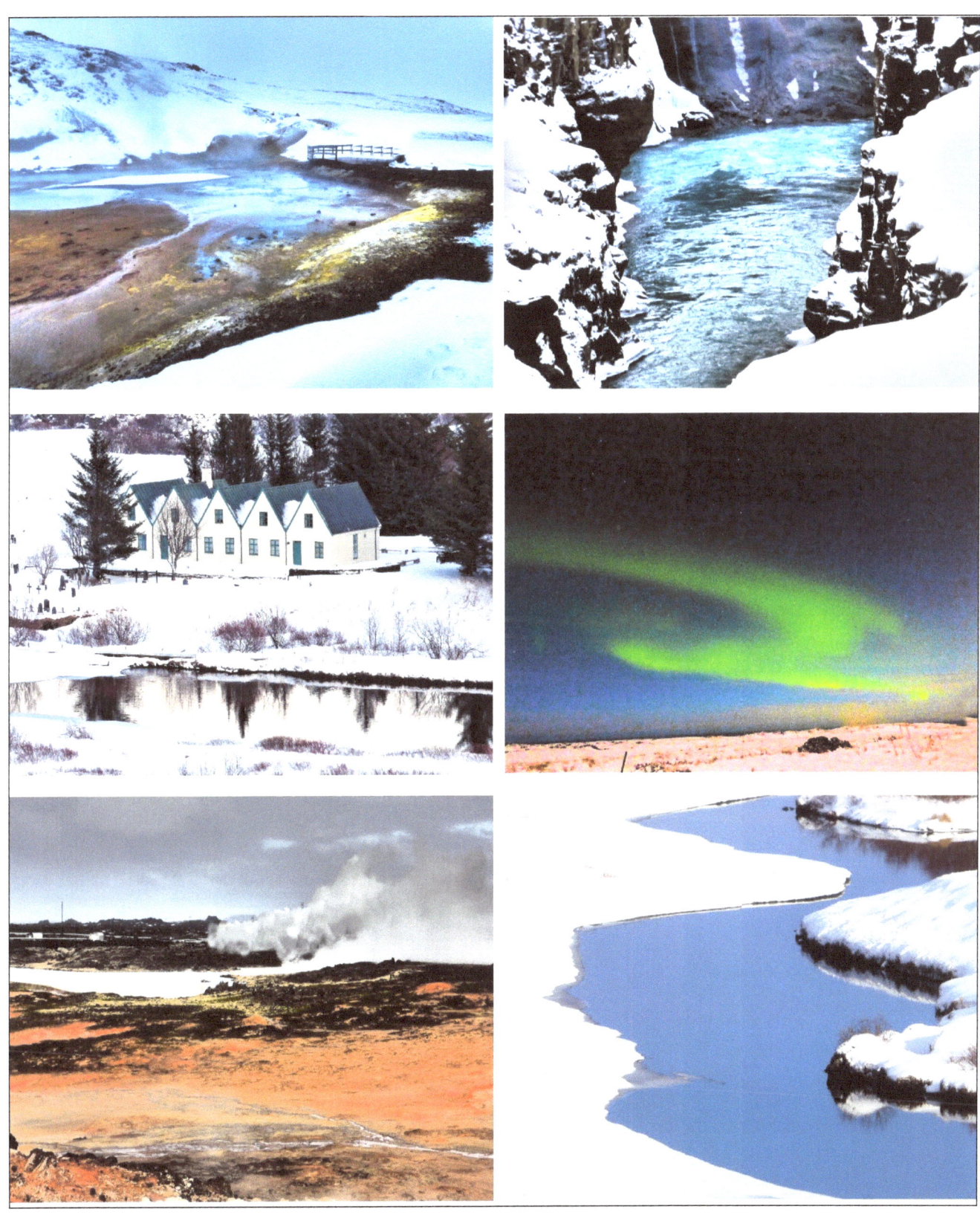

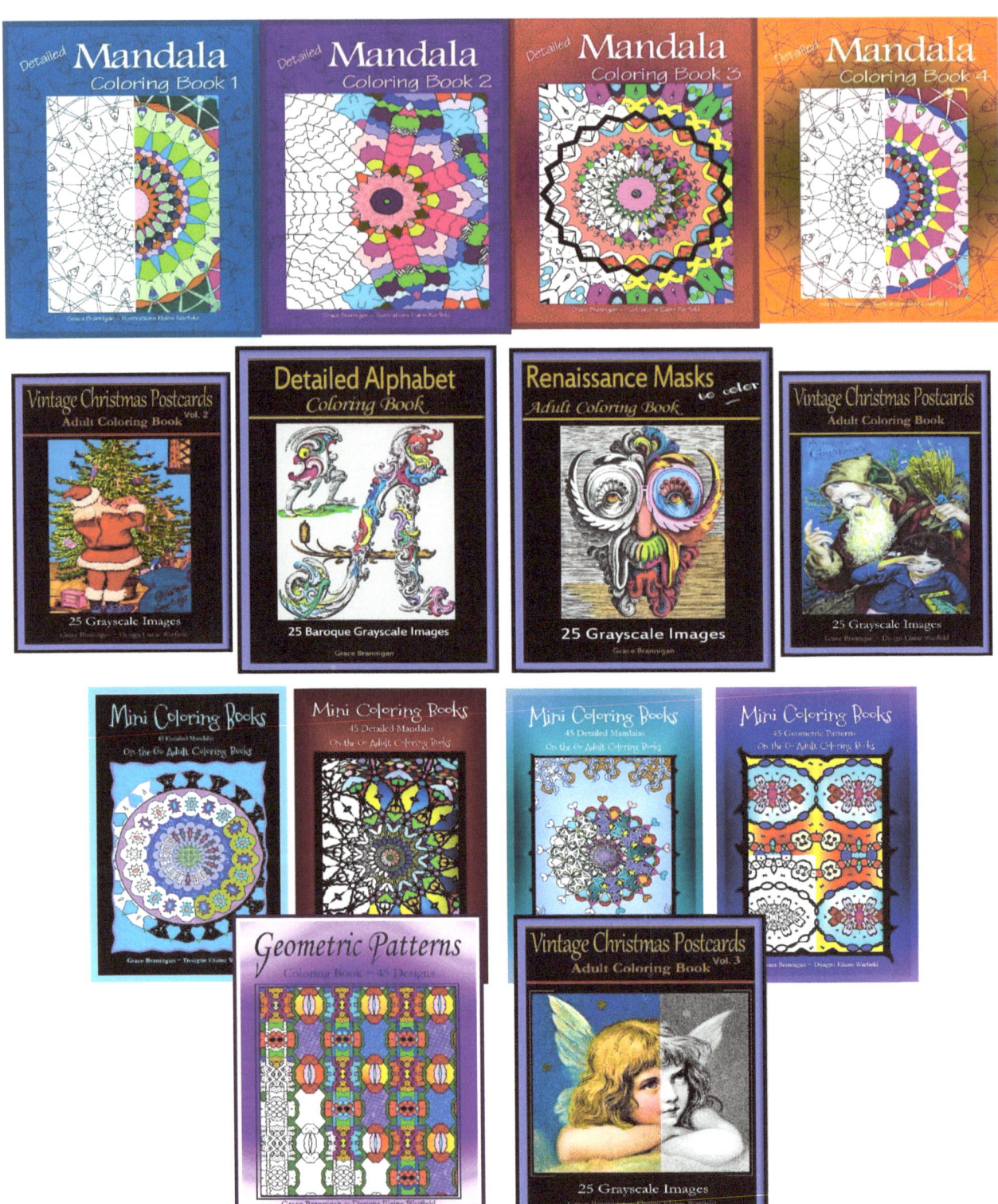

I hope you enjoyed coloring these grayscale photographs. Please leave a review on Amazon, as it helps the author and buyers. Check my website for all coloring books, journals and sketchbooks!

Website: http://www.ColoringBooksForAdults.info

Facebook: Coloring Books For Adults Info

Twitter: @ColoringAdults

www.ingramcontent.com/pod-product-compliance
Lightning Source LLC
Chambersburg PA
CBHW050806180526
45159CB00004B/1566